W9-AED-496

This Coloring Book belongs to:

_____

Coloring Book

Impressionism

PRESTEL

Munich · Berlin · London · New York

The Impressionists

were a group of artists who lived about 130 years ago in Paris,

the capital of France,

and invented a new kind of painting.

These artists no longer worked in their studios but

took their paints, canvases, and easels outdoors to paint.

They painted the colorful life of Paris and the landscape around it

and how these changed at different times of day and during different sesons.

They captured the impressions of the moment in pictures full of light and color:

the midday sun's golden spots of light falling through the foliage,

the warm colors of the evening light on the houses,

the cool blue of snow-covered landscapes,

the gray mood of rain, the shimmering colors of a dancer's clothing.

In this book you'll find pictures by the famous Impressionists that you can color in
and draw on.

Use the colors you find most beautiful and paint the pictures
any way you want!

Noon in the park ...
          would you like to add something?

Paint or draw a landscape for the windmill.

Claude Monet liked to paint the river landscape from his boat.

Where are they going?

A ballet class practicing—draw or paint more and color the picture!

Draw or paint more horses training at the racetrack!

What's going on in the streets?

The light bathes the haystack in warm colors. Would you like to finish Monet's picture?

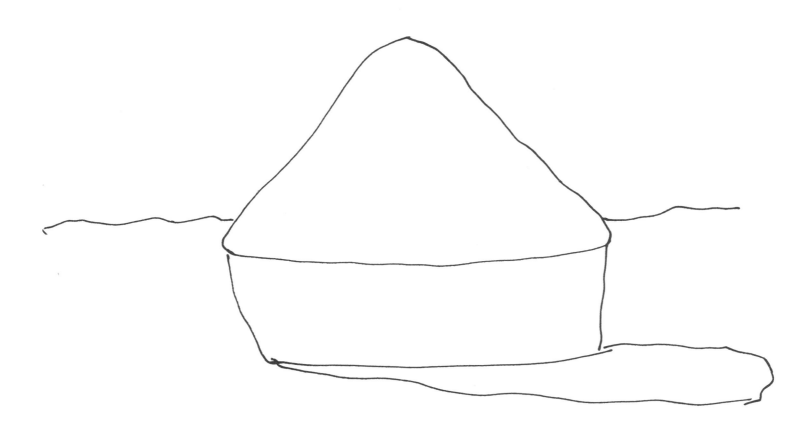

This is what haystacks look like when they're lit up by the warm evening light.

What do the colors look like in the blue light of morning?

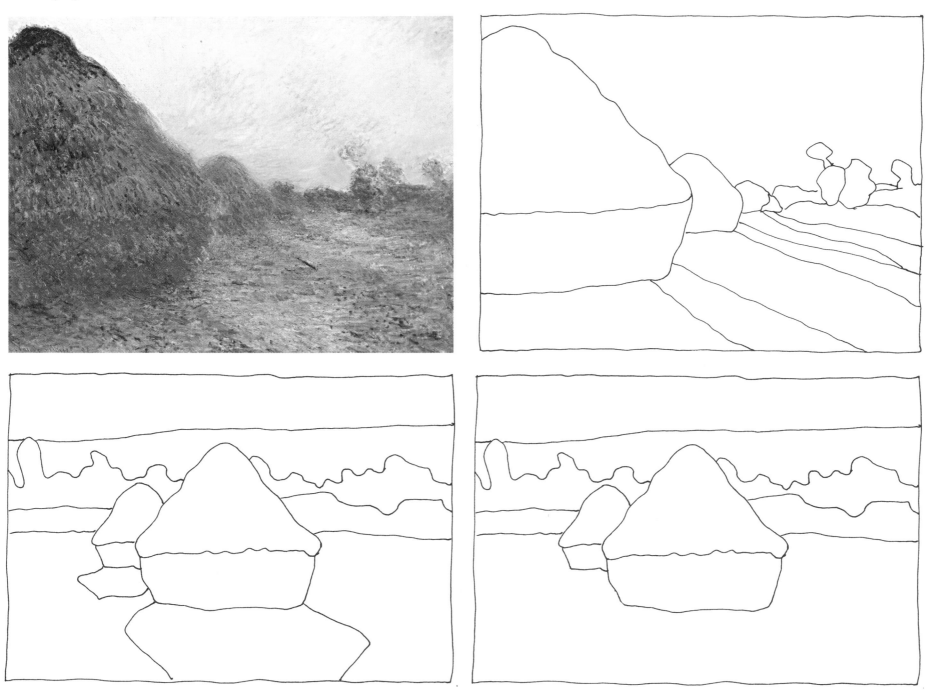

... in the rain?

... in winter?

A happy dance in colorful clothing ...

A celebration!

The little girl wants to water the flowers. Paint or draw a garden for her!

Look carefully: These pictures are made up of many tiny dots of color.
Can you do that too?

Would you like to finish the picture?

The original pictures

Here are the pictures that served as models for this book.
Do you recognize any of them?

Camille Pissarro (1830–1903)
1 Windmill at Knocke (Belgium), 1894.
Private collection (Photo: Artothek)

Edouard Manet (1832–1883)
2 Boating, 1874. New York, Metropolitan
Museum of Art (Photo: akg)
3 Claude Monet Working on his Boat in
Argenteuil, 1874. Munich, Neue Pinakothek
(Photo: Artothek)

Edgar Degas (1834–1917)
4 Dance Class, around 1871. New York,
Metropolitan Museum of Art (Photo: Artothek)
5 Breaking-In, around 1880. Moscow, Puschkin
Museum (Photo: Artothek)

Alfred Sisley (1839–1899)
6 Square in Argenteuil, 1872.
Paris, Musée d'Orsay

Claude Monet (1840–1926)
7 The Terrace at Sainte-Adresse, 1867.
New York, The Metropolitan Museum of Art
(Photo: Artothek)
8 Haystacks, 1890–91. Private collection
9 Haystacks, 1890–91. Private collection
10 Haystacks: Snow Effect, 1890–91. Edinburgh,
National Gallery of Scotland

Pierre-Auguste Renoir (1841–1919)
11 Dance at Bougival, 1883. Boston,
Museum of Fine Arts
12 Dance in the Country, around 1883. Paris,
Musée d'Orsay

13 Dance in the City, 1882. Paris, Musée d'Orsay
14 Dance at Le Moulin de la Galette, 1876. Paris,
Musée d'Orsay (Photo: Artothek)
15 A Girl with a Watering Can, 1876.
Washington, National Gallery (Photo: Artothek)

Georges Seurat (1859–1891)
16 A Sunday Afternoon on the Island of La
Grande Jatte, 1884–85. Chicago, Art Institute
(Photo: Artothek)

Paul Signac (1863–1935)
17 Antibes, Evening, 1914. Strasbourg,
Musée des Beaux-Arts de la Ville

© Prestel Verlag
Munich · Berlin · London · New York, 2010.
2nd printing 2010

Prestel, a member of Verlagsgruppe Random House GmbH

Prestel Verlag, Munich
www.prestel.de

Prestel Publishing Ltd.
4 Bloomsbury Place
London WC1A 2QA

Prestel Publishing
900 Broadway, Suite 603
New York, NY 10003

www.prestel.com

The series title, conception, and presentation of the series
Coloring Books is protected by the laws of copyright and
competition law.

Concept, drawings, and texts: Doris Kutschbach
Translation: Cynthia Hall
Design: Andrea Mogwitz, Munich
Production: Nele Krüger, Selen Bulut
Lithography: ReproLine mediateam, Munich
Printing and binding: Těšínká Tiskárna, Český Těšín

Printed on acid-free paper by Papier Union GmbH,
Germany.

ISBN 978-3-7913-3792-0